Robert Burns

The Scottish Bard

First published in Great Britain by Brockhampton Press,
a member of the Hodder Headline Group,
20 Bloomsbury Street, London WC1B 3QA.

This 1999 edition is published by Gramercy Books™, an imprint of
Random House Value Publishing, Inc., 201 East 50th Street, New York, N.Y. 10022.

Gramercy Books™ and colophon are trademarks of
Random House Value Publishing, Inc.

Random House
New York • Toronto • London • Sydney • Auckland
http://www.randomhouse.com/

Created and produced by Flame Tree Publishing,
part of The Foundry Creative Media Company Limited,
Crabtree Hall, Crabtree Lane, Fulham, London SW6 6TY.

Special thanks to
Kate Brown and Kelley Doak for their work on this series.

Printed and bound in U. A. E.

A CIP catalog record for this book is available from the Library of Congress.

ISBN 0-517-16100-1

8 7 6 5 4 3 2 1

Robert Burns

The Scottish Bard

Selected and Written by
O. B. DUANE

Gramercy Books
New York

Contents

Introduction

ROBERT Burns is Scotland's most venerated poet, a man whose popularity is still on the increase two centuries after his verses first appeared. Above all other Scottish poets, Burns continues to enjoy the privileged status of national muse, for it was largely through his poetry and songs that Scotland's cultural identity was restored to life and her language and lore preserved. Burns's deep love of his country fired his ambition to write in the Scottish vernacular, resulting in the creation of a unique brand of poetry, full of character, integrity, humour, satire and lyrical harmony. His was not a lofty understanding of the poet's role; he believed in the realistic and honest treatment of subject and in the search for universal meaning in the commonplace. He considered song equally important to poetry and his knowledge of folk music was unrivalled. During his lifetime, he energetically gathered together and amended well over two hundred songs covering every facet of eighteenth-century Scottish life. The importance of his contribution to Scotland's literary tradition is beyond measure, but every year on the anniversary of his birth it is fervently acknowledged in the celebrations and poetry readings that take place not just in his native country, but throughout the world.

Robert, the eldest of seven children, was born in a two-roomed clay-cottage in the village of Alloway, about two miles from the town of Ayr in south-west Scotland. His father, William Burnes, was a simple farmer, yet also a relatively progressive and individual character who was determined that his children should be well-educated. His mother, Agnes Broun, was an uncomplicated, uneducated woman, but an excellent wife and mother who ran a happy household in

spite of the hardship and poverty they were all forced to endure. Robert's early education was provided by John Murdoch, a competent young tutor hired by his father and four other neighbours when the school at Alloway Mill was forced to close in early 1765. This formal education came to an abrupt end the following year, however, once the family moved to the moorland farm of 'Mount Oliphant'. Their father decided to continue the boys' education himself and he taught them geography and ancient history and also encouraged them to read. In time, Robert became familiar with classic authors from Shakespeare onwards, and encountered the works of various poets in collections that occasionally passed through the household. An important influence on the development of his creative imagination at this early stage was an old friend of his mother's, Betsy Davidson, whom Burns later described as someone with 'the largest collection in the country of tales and songs concerning devils, ghosts, fairies, brownies, witches, warlocks, spunkies, kelpies, elf-candles, dead-lights, wraiths, apparitions, cantraips, enchanted towers, giants, and other trumpery'. It was this catalogue of imagery, firmly planted in his memory, that Burns later drew on when he wrote 'Tam o' Shanter', the poem that most pleased him.

At fifteen, Robert first 'committed the sin of rhyme', and wrote 'O once I lov'd a Bonie Lass'. There was, however, little opportunity for creativity of any sort while he remained the principal labourer on the farm. 'Mount Oliphant' was a desolate place offering little or no society with other people. Even before he grew to adolescence, Burns suffered fits of depression, brought on by his sombre and daunting life, and these would occur frequently throughout his adulthood.

In 1775 he attended a school in Kirkoswald where he made good progress with his studies and took full advantage of the vibrant life of the village, learning for the first time to 'take his glass'. But he could not remain in Kirkoswald longer than a few months, since his father was now in severe financial difficulties. By 1777, William Burnes had decided to abandon Mount Oliphant and moved his family to the larger, yet more fertile farm of 'Lochlea' in Tarbolton parish. Circumstances improved for a time at Lochlea and Robert began to enjoy a more active social life. By 1881, he had become a Freemason and had founded a debating club, sharpening his instinctive wit and developing those powers of conversation that were later to impress Edinburgh's aristocracy. Burns was not especially creative during this period, but it was at about this time that he encountered the vernacular, slightly irreverent, verse of Robert Fergusson which had a powerful influence on him. He had almost given up the thought of writing poetry, he later wrote, 'but meeting with Fergusson's Scotch poems, I strung anew my wildly-sounding rustic lyre with emulating vigour'.

When his father died in 1784, Burns moved the family to the smaller farm of 'Mossgiel' in the adjoining parish of Mauchline. He had begun his *Commonplace Book* the previous year, a journal containing his first serious literary efforts. By now a grown man longing to make his mark, he began to draw attention to himself as a champion of liberal clergymen against the 'Old Lights'. His poetic style matured dramatically at the same time and it was at Mossgiel that he produced the majority of his best known work, including 'The Twa Dogs', 'To a Mouse', 'Scotch Drink', 'Halloween', 'The Cotter's Saturday Night', 'Address to a Deil' and 'The Ordination'. 'The Twa Dogs' was evidently inspired by his father's bitter experience of landlords and the wretched circumstances of poverty leading to his death. 'Holy Willie's Prayer'* presented a scathing attack on the church's 'Old Lights', and was followed by 'The Holy Fair' in the autumn of 1785, a poem describing the hypocrisy and debauchery of the great religious festivals held around Communion time.

Burn's first volume of verse, *Poems Chiefly in the Scottish Dialect*, was published in Kilmarnock in July 1786. At the time of its publication, his personal life, not for the first, or indeed the last time, was in deep turmoil and he was resolved to emigrate to Jamaica. He had met and fallen in love with Jean Armour in 1784 and she was now carrying his child. Burns wanted to marry Jean and the two signed a document pledging themselves to each other, but her father would not allow the match and sent her away to stay with relatives. Burns published his poems partly to raise funds for his departure, but they were an immediate success and he was

persuaded to abandon all thoughts of Jamaica, and instead to travel to Edinburgh with a view to the publication of a new edition of his verses.

The twenty-seven-year-old poet was immediately popular in the Scottish capital. His gregarious, unaffected personality fascinated Edinburgh's élite society and he won many influential friends. He was introduced to William Creech, one of the best-known publishers and literary agents, who undertook to publish the Edinburgh edition of Burns's poems. He was also asked by James Johnson to help collect old Scottish songs for *The Scots Musical Museum*, a request to which he responded with great enthusiasm. Between 1787 and 1792, he contributed over 140 songs to Johnson's collections, refusing all money for this work which he considered his patriotic duty.

Furnished with the sum of about five hundred pounds from the Edinburgh edition of his verses, Burns returned to Mossgiel in February of 1788 and married Jean Armour. He wanted to follow a career which would allow him to write poetry yet provide a comfortable living. He took a farm in Dumfriesshire called 'Ellisland' in 1788, but decided also to train as an excise officer in case farming proved unprofitable. Ellisland turned out to be a bad bargain, and by November 1791, he had quit farming and moved to Dumfries where he took up full-time work as an exciseman.

While working at this profession, Burns continued to contribute songs to Johnson's *Musical Museum*, and in the autumn of 1790 he composed 'Tam o'Shanter', which many critics consider his masterpiece. In August 1792, he received a letter from George Thomson in Edinburgh, inviting him to take part in a new collection of Scottish songs, *Select Collection of Original Scottish Airs*. From 1793 onwards, he was almost entirely absorbed in song-revision and by June of that year the first volume of Thomson's collection had appeared, including the twenty-five songs which Burns had promised.

In the spring of 1775, Burns complained to his friend Maria Riddel that he was 'so ill as to be scarce able to hold this miserable pen to this miserable paper'. Later that September, his daughter Elizabeth died and Burns was heartbroken. Weakened by his bereavement and many severe bouts of illness over the years, he had neither the energy nor the will to fight off an attack of rheumatic illness that winter. He lingered on in great pain until his death in July at the age of only thirty-seven, but by then he had prepared himself for the end and met death calmly and peacefully.

Author's Note

The poems and songs in this volume have been reproduced from Professor James Kinsley's *Burns Poems and Songs* (Oxford University Press, 1969). Words such as 'hell' and 'damned', which originally appeared in dashes, have been spelled out here to make the text more accessible. A glossary is also included explaining words in Scottish dialect which may be unfamiliar to the reader.

*'Holy Willie's Prayer', although written between 1784-85, was not included in the Kilmarnock edition published in 1786, because it was considered too offensive.

Chronology

1759   Robert Burns is born on 25 January in Alloway, Ayrshire, to William Burnes and Agnes Broun.

1766   The family move to a seventy acre farm with poor prospects, Mount Oliphant.

1772   Robert attends Dalrymphle school during the summer.

1774   He writes his first song, 'O Once I Lov'd', during the autumn.

1777   The family move again to a larger farm 'Lochlea', near Tarbolton.

1782   Burns returns to 'Lochlea' after the shop at Irvine burns to the ground.

1783   He begins to record and revise his early poems in his *First Commonplace Book*.

1784   Burns meets and falls in love with Jean Armour.

1785   Burns's first child by his mother'servant, Betty Paton is born. She is named Elizabeth. He transcribes his first Scottish vernacular poem, *The Death and Dying Words of Poor Mailie* into the *First Commonplace Book*.

1786   Jean Armour becomes pregnant by Burns. He books his passage for Jamaica but postpones it when *Poems Chiefly in the Scottish Dialect* is published at Kilmarnock. Jean Armour gives birth to twins.

1787   An enlarged edition of *Poems Chiefly in the Scottish Dialect* is published in April. The first volume of James Johnson's *Scots Musical Museum* is published, including three songs by Burns. Jenny Clow gives birth to his baby.

1788   A second volume of *Scots Musical Museum* is published,
        including thirty-two songs by Burns. Jean Armour
        gives birth to twin girls but they die within a
        month. Burns acknowledges her as his wife. He is
        commissioned as an exciseman.

1789   Burns's son, Francis Wallace, is born.

1790   The third volume of *Scots Musical Museum* is
        published, including forty songs by Burns. The
        poet completes *Tam o' Shanter* in honour of Captain
        Grose in the autumn.

1791   A daughter Elizabeth is born to Helen Ann Park.
        Jean takes in the infant.

1792   A fourth volume of *Scots Musical Museum* is published.
        Burns contributes songs to George Thomson's *Select
        Collection of Original Scottish Airs*. A daughter Elizabeth is
        born to Jean.

1793   A new edition of *Poems Chiefly in the Scottish Dialect* is
        published, expanded into two volumes.

1794   A son, James Glencairn, is born. Burns is appointed
        acting supervisor of the Excise.

1795   His daughter Elizabeth dies shortly before her third
        birthday. Burns becomes seriously ill with
        rheumatic fever.

1796   He dies on 21 July. He is buried on 25 July and on
        this day Jean gives birth to their son Maxwell. A
        fifth volume of *Scots Musical Museum* is published in
        December, including thirty-seven songs by Burns,
        among them 'Auld Lang Syne'.

O Once I Lov'd

O ONCE I lov'd a bonnie lass,
An' aye I love her still,
An' whilst that virtue warms my breast
I'll love my handsome Nell.

As bonnie lasses I hae seen,
And mony full as braw,
But for a modest gracefu' mein
The like I never saw.

A bonny lass I will confess,
Is pleasant to the e'e,
But without some better qualities
She's no a lass for me.

But Nelly's looks are blythe and sweet,
And what is best of a',
Her reputation is compleat,
And fair without a flaw;

She dresses ay sae clean and neat,
Both decent and genteel;
And then there's something in her gait
Gars ony dress look weel.

A gaudy dress and gentle air
May slightly touch the heart,
But it's innocence and modesty
That polishes the dart.

'Tis this in Nelly pleases me,
'Tis this enchants my soul;
For absolutely in my breast
She reigns without controul.

Winter, A Dirge

I

THE WINTRY West extends his blast,
And hail and rain does blaw;
Or, the stormy North sends driving forth,
The blinding sleet and snaw:
While, tumbling brown, the Burn comes down,
And roars frae bank to brae;
And bird and beast, in covert, rest,
And pass the heartless day.

II

'The sweeping blast, the sky o'ercast,'
The joyless *winter-day*,
Let others fear, to me more dear,
Than all the pride of May:
The Tempest's howl, it *soothes* my soul,
My *griefs* it seems to join;
The leafless trees my fancy please,
Their *fate* resembles mine!

III

Thou pow'r supreme, whose mighty Scheme
These *woes* of mine fulfil;
Here, firm, I rest, they *must* be best,
Because they are *Thy* Will!
Then all I want (Oh, do thou grant
This one request of mine!)
Since to *enjoy* Thou dost deny,
Assist me to *resign* !

The Death and Dying Words of Poor Mailie, The Author's only Pet Yowe, An Unco Mournfu' Tale

AS MAILIE, an' her lambs thegither,
Was ae day nibbling on the tether,
Upon her cloot she coost a hitch,
An' owre she warsl'd in the ditch:
There, groaning, dying, she did ly,
When Hughoc he cam doytan by.

Wi' glowrin een, an' lifted han's,
Poor Hughoc like a statue stan's;
He saw her days were near hand ended,
But, waes my heart! he could na mend it!
He gaped wide, but naething spak,
At length poor Mailie silence brak.

'O thou, whase lamentable face
Appears to mourn my woefu' case!
My dying words attentive hear,
An' bear them to my Master dear.

Tell him, if e'er again he keep
As muckle gear as buy a sheep,
O, bid him never tye them mair,
Wi' wicked strings o' hemp or hair!

But ca' them out to park or hill,
An' let them wander at their will:
So, may his flock increase an' grow
To *scores* o' lambs, an' *packs* of woo'!

Tell him, he was a Master kin',
An' ay was guid to me an' mine;
An' now my *dying* charge I gie him,
My helpless *lambs*, I trust them wi' him.

O, bid him save their harmless lives,
Frae dogs an' tods, an' butchers' knives!
But gie them guid *cow-milk* their fill,
Till they be fit to fend themsel;
An' tent them duely, e'en an' morn,
Wi' taets o' *hay* an' ripps o' *corn*.

An' may they never learn the gaets,
Of ither vile, wanrestfu' *Pets*!
To slink thro' slaps, an' reave an' steal,
At stacks o' pease, or stocks o' kail.
So may they, like their great *forbears*,
For monie a year come thro' the sheers:
So *wives* will gie them bits o' bread,
An' *bairns* greet for them when they're dead.

My poor *toop-lamb*, my son an' heir,
O, bid him breed him up wi' care!
An' if he live to be a beast,
To pit some havins in his breast!
An' warn him, what I winna name,
To stay content wi' *yowes* at hame;
An' no to rin an' wear his cloots,
Like ither menseless, graceless brutes.

An' niest my *yowie*, silly thing,
Gude keep thee frae a *tether string*!
O, may thou ne'er forgather up,
Wi' onie blastet, moorlan *toop*;
Buy ay keep mind to moop an' mell,
Wi' sheep o' credit like thysel!

And now, *my bairns*, wi' my last breath,
I lae'e my blessin wi' you baith:
An' when ye think upo' your Mither,
Mind to be kind to ane anither.
Now, honest *Hughoc*, dinna fail,
To tell my Master a' my tale;
An' bid him burn this cursed *tether*,
An' for thy pains thou'se get my blather.'

This said, poor *Mailie* turn'd her head,
An' clos'd her een amang the dead!

Mary Morison (A Song)

O MARY, at thy window be,
It is the wish'd, the trysted hour;
Those smiles and glances let me see,
That make the miser's treasure poor:
How blythely wad I bide the stoure,
A weary slave frae sun to sun;
Could I the rich reward secure,
The lovely Mary Morison!

Yestreen when to the trembling string
The dance gaed through the lighted ha',
To thee my fancy took its wing,
I sat, but neither heard, nor saw:
Though this was fair, and that was braw,
And yon the toast of a' the town,
I sigh'd, and said amang them a',
'Ye are na Mary Morison.'

O Mary, canst thou wreck his peace,
What for thy sake wad gladly die!
Or canst thou break that heart of his,
Whase only faute is loving thee!
If love for love thou wilt na gie,
At least be pity to me shown;
A thought ungentle canna be
The thought o' Mary Morison.

Green Grow the Rashes.
A FRAGMENT

Green grow the rashes, O;
Green grow the rashes, O;
The sweetest hours that e'er I spend,
Are spent amang the lasses, O.

I
THERE'S nought but care on ev'ry han',
In ev'ry hour that passes, O:
What signifies the life o' man,
An' 'twere na for the lasses, O.

Green grow, &c.

II
The warly race may riches chase,
An' riches still may fly them, O;
An' tho' at last they catch them fast,
Their hearts can ne'er enjoy them, O.

Green grow, &c.

III
But gie me a canny hour at e'en,
My arms about my Dearie, O;
An' warly cares, an' warly men,
May a' gae tapsalteerie, O!

Green grow, &c.

IV

For you sae douse, ye sneer at this,
Ye're nought but senseless asses, O:
The wisest Man the warl' saw,
He dearly lov'd the lasses, O.

Green grow, &c.

V

Auld Nature swears, the lovely Dears
Her noblest work she classes, O:
Her prentice han' she try'd on man,
An' then she made the lasses, O.

Green grow, &c.

Holy Willie's Prayer

And send the Godly in a pet to pray —
POPE.

O THOU that in the heavens does dwell!
Wha, as it pleases best thysel,
Sends ane to heaven an' ten to hell
A' for thy glory!
And no for ony gude or ill
They've done before thee.—

I bless and praise thy matchless might,
When thousands thou has left in night,
That I am here before thy sight,
For gifts and grace
A burning and a shining light
To a' this place.—

What was I, or my generation,
That I should get such exaltation?
I, wha deserv'd most just damnation,
For broken laws
Sax thousand years ere my creation,
Thro' Adam's cause!

When from my mother's womb I fell,
Thou might hae plung'd me deep in hell,
To gnash my gooms, and weep, and wail
In burning lakes,
Whare damned devils roar and yell
Chain'd to their stakes.—

Yet I am here, a chosen sample,
To show thy grace is great and ample:
I'm here, a pillar o' thy temple,
　　Strong as a rock,
A guide, a ruler, and example
　　To a' thy flock.—

[O Lord thou kens what zeal I bear,
When drinkers drink, and swearers swear,
And singin' there, and dancin' here,
　　Wi' great an' sma';
For I am keepet by thy fear,
　　Free frae them a'.—]

But yet—O Lord—confess I must—
At times I'm fash'd wi' fleshy lust;
And sometimes, too, in warldly trust
　　Vile Self gets in;
But thou remembers we are dust,
　　Defiled wi' sin.—

O Lord—yestreen—thou kens—wi' Meg —
Thy pardon I sincerely beg!
O, may 't ne'er be a living plague,
　　To my dishounour!
An' I'll ne'er lift a lawless leg
　　Again upon her.—

Besides, I farther maun avow,
Wi' Leezie's lass, three times—I trow—
But Lord, that Friday I was fou
　　When I cam near her;
Or else, thou kens, thy servant true
　　Wad never steer her.—

Maybe thou lets this fleshly thorn
Buffet thy servant e'en and morn,
Lest he o're proud and high should turn
That he's sae gifted;
If sae, thy han'maun e'en be borne
Untill thou lift it.—

Lord bless thy Chosen in this place,
For here thou has a chosen race:
But God confound their stubborn face,
And blast their name,
What bring thy rulers to disgrace
And open shame.—

Lord, mind Gaun Hamilton's deserts!
He drinks, and swears, and plays at cartes,
Yet has sae mony taking arts
Wi' Great and Sma',
Frae God's ain priest the people's hearts
He steals awa.—

And when we chasten'd him therefore,
Thou kens how he bred sic a splore,
And set the warld in a roar
O' laughin at us:
Curse thou his basket and his store,
Kail and potatoes.—

Lord, hear my earnest cry and prayer
Against that Presbytry of Ayr!
Thy strong right hand, Lord, make it bare
Upon their heads!
Lord, visit them, and dinna spare,
For their misdeeds!

O Lord—my God, that glib-tongu'd Aiken!
My very heart and flesh are quaking
To think how I sat sweating, shaking,
    An' p-ss'd wi' dread,
While Auld wi' hingin lip gaed sneaking
    And hid his head!

Lord—in thy day o' vengeance try him!
Lord visit him that did employ him!
And pass not in thy mercy by them,
    Nor hear their prayer,
But for thy people's sake destroy them,
    And dinna spare!

But Lord, remember me and mine
Wi' mercies temporal and divine!
That I for grace and gear may shine,
    Excell'd by nane!
And a' the glory shall be thine!
    AMEN! AMEN!

To a Mouse, On turning her up in her Nest, with the Plough, November, 1785

WEE, sleeket, cowran, tim'rous *beastie*,
O, what a panic's in thy breastie!
Thou need na start awa sae hasty,
Wi' bickering brattle!
I wad be laith to rin an' chase thee,
Wi' murd'ring *pattle*!

I'm truly sorry Man's dominion
Has broken Nature's social union,
An' justifies that ill opinion,
Which makes thee startle,
At me, thy poor, earth-born companion,
An' *fellow-mortal*!

I doubt na, whyles, but thou may *thieve*;
What then? poor beastie, thou maun live!
A *daimen-icker* in a *thrave*
'S a sma' request:
I'll get a blessin wi' the lave,
An' never miss't!

Thy wee-bit *housie*, too, in ruin!
It's silly wa's the win's are strewin!
An' naething, now, to big a new ane,
O' foggage green!
An' bleak *December's winds* ensuin,
Baith snell an' keen!

Thou saw the fields laid bare an' wast,
An' weary *Winter* comin fast,
An' cozie here, beneath the blast,
Thou thought to dwell,
Till crash! the cruel *coulter* past
Out thro' thy cell.

That wee-bit heap o' leaves an' stibble,
Has cost thee monie a weary nibble!
Now thou's turn'd out, for a' thy trouble,
But house or hald,
To thole the Winter's *sleety dribble*,
An' *cranreuch* cauld!

But Mousie, thou art no thy-lane,
In proving *foresight* may be vain:
The best laid schemes o' *Mice* an' *Men*,
Gang aft agley,
An' lea'e us nought but grief an' pain,
For promis'd joy!

Still, thou art blest, compar'd wi' *me*!
The *present* only toucheth thee:
But Och! I *backward* cast my e'e,
On prospects drear!
An' *forward*, tho' I canna *see*,
I *guess* an' *fear*!

The Twa Dogs. A Tale

'TWAS IN that place o' *Scotland's* isle,
That bears the name o' auld king COIL,
Upon a bonie day in June,
When wearing thro' the afternoon,
Twa Dogs, that were na thrang at hame,
Forgather'd ance upon a time.

The first I'll name, they ca'd him *Ceasar*,
Was keepet for his Honor's pleasure;
His hair, his size, his mouth, his lugs,
Show'd he was nane o' Scotland's dogs,
But whalpet some place far abroad,
Whare sailors gang to fish for Cod.

His locked, letter'd, braw brass-collar,
Show'd him the *gentleman* an' *scholar*;
But tho' he was o' high degree,
The fient a pride na pride had he,
But wad hae spent an hour caressan,
Ev'n wi' a Tinkler-gipsey's *messan*:
At *Kirk* or *Market*, *Mill* or *Smiddie*,
Nae tawtied *tyke*, tho' e'er sae duddie,
But he wad stan't, as glad to see him,
An' stroan't on stanes an' hillocks wi' him.

The tither was a *ploughman's collie*,
A rhyming, ranting, raving billie,
Wha for his friend an' comrade had him,
And in his freaks had *Luath* ca'd him,
After some dog in *Highlan Sang*,
Was made lang syne, lord knows how lang.

He was a gash an' faithfu' *tyke*,
As ever lap a sheugh, or dyke!
His honest, sonsie, baws'nt *face*,
Ay gat him friends in ilka place;
His *breast* was white, his towzie *back*,
Weel clad wi' coat o' glossy black;
His gawsie tail, wi' upward curl,
Hung owre his hurdies wi' a swirl.

Nae doubt but they were fain o' ither,
An' unco pack an' thick the gither;
Wi' social *nose* whyles snuff'd an' snowcket;
Whyles mice an' modewurks they howcket;
Whyles scour'd awa in lang excursion,
An' worry'd ither in *diversion*;
Untill wi' daffin weary grown,
Upon a knowe they sat them down,
An' there began a lang digression
About the *lords o' the creation.*

CEASAR
I've aften wonder'd, honest *Luath*,
What sort o' life poor dogs like you have;
An' when the *gentry's* life I saw,
What way *poor bodies* liv'd ava.

Our *Laird* gets in his racked rents,
His coals, his kane, an' a' his stents;
He rises when he likes himsel;
His flunkies answer at the bell;
He ca's his coach; he ca's his horse;
He draws a bonie, silken purse
As lang's my *tail*, whare thro' the steeks,
The yellow, letter'd *Geordie* keeks.
Frae morn to een it's nought but toiling,

At baking, roasting, frying, boiling:
An' tho' the gentry first are steghan,
Yet e'en the *ha' folk* fill their peghan
Wi' sauce, ragouts, an' sic like trashtrie,
That's little short o' downright wastrie.
Our *Whipper-in*, wee, blastiet wonner,
Poor, worthless elf, it eats a dinner,
    Better than ony *Tenant-man*
    His Honor has in a' the lan':
And what poor *Cot-folk* pit their painch in,
I own it's past my comprehension.—

LUATH
Trowth, *Ceasar*, whyles they're fash'd eneugh;
    A *Cotter* howckan in a sheugh,
    Wi' dirty stanes biggan an dyke,
    Bairan a quarry, an' sic like,
    Himsel, a wife, he thus sustains,
    A smytrie o' wee, duddie weans,
An' nought but his han'-daurk, to keep
    Them right an' tight in *thack an' raep*.

An' when they meet wi' sair disasters,
Like loss o' health, or want o' masters,
Ye maist wad think, a wee touch langer,
An' they maun starve o' cauld an' hunger:
But how it comes, I never kent yet,
They're maistly wonderfu' contented;
An' buirdly chiels, an' clever hizzies,
    Are bred in sic a way as this is.

CEASAR

But then, to see how ye're negleket,
How huff'd, an' cuff'd, an' disrespeket!
Lord man, our gentry care as little
  For *delvers, ditchers*, an' sic cattle;
They gang as saucy by poor folk,
  As I wad by a stinkan brock.

I've notic'd, on our Laird's *court-day*,
An' mony a time my heart's been wae,
  Poor *tenant-bodies*, scant o' cash,
  How they maun thole a *factor's* snash;
He'll stamp an' threaten, curse an' swear,
He'll *apprehend* them, *poind* their gear'
While they maun stand, wi' aspect humble,
  An' hear it a', an' fear an' tremble!

I see how folk live that hae riches,
But surely poor-folk maun be *wretches*!

LUATH

They're no sae wretched's ane wad think;
  Tho' constantly on poortith's brink
  They're sae accustom'd wi' the sight,
  The view o't gies them little fright.

Then chance an' fortune are sae guided,
  They're ay in less or mair provided;
An' tho' fatigu'd wi' close employment,
  A blink o' rest's a sweet enjoyment.

The dearest comfort o' their lives,
Their grushie weans an' faithfu' wives;
The *prattling things* are just their pride,
That sweetens a' their fire-side.

An' whyles, twalpennie-worth o' *nappy*
Can mak the bodies unco happy;
They lay aside their private cares,
To mind the Kirk and State affairs;
They'll talk o' *patronage* an' *priests*,
Wi' kindling fury i' their breasts,
Or tell what new taxation's comin,
An' ferlie at the folk in LON'ON.

As bleak-fac'd Hallowmass returns,
They get the jovial, rantan *Kirns*,
When *rural life*, of ev'ry station,
Unite in common recreation;
Love blinks, Wit slaps, an' social Mirth
Forgets there's *care* upo' the earth.

That *merry day* the year begins,
They bar the door on frosty win's;
The nappy reeks wi' mantling ream,
An' sheds a heart-inspiring steam;
The luntan pipe, an' sneeshin mill,
Are handed round wi' right guid will;
The cantie, auld folks, crackan crouse,
The young anes rantan thro' house—
My heart has been sae fain to see them,
That I for joy hae *barket* wi' them.

Still it's owre true that ye hae said,
Sic game is now owre aften play'd;
  There's monie a creditable *stock*
  O' decent, honest, fawsont folk,
Are riven out baith root an' branch,
Some rascal's pridefu' greed to quench,
  Wha thinks to knit himsel the faster
    In favor wi' some *gentle Master*,
  Wha, aiblins thrang a *parliamentin*,
  For *Britain's guid* his saul indentin—

CEASAR
  Haith lad, ye little ken about it;
  For *Britain's guid*! guid faith! I doubt it.
Say rather, gaun as PREMIERS lead him,
An' saying *aye* or *no's* they bid him:
  At operas an' Plays parading,
Mortgaging, gambling, masquerading:
    Or maybe, in a frolic daft,
  To HAGUE or CALAIS takes a waft,
  To make a *tour* an' take a whirl,
  To learn *bon ton* an' see the worl'.

  There at VIENNA or VERSAILLES,
  He rives his father's auld entails;
  Or by MADRID he takes the rout,
To thrum *guittarres* an' fecht wi' *nowt*;
    Or down *Italian Vista* startles,
Wh-re-hunting amang groves o' myrtles:
  Then bowses drumlie *German-water*,
  To make himsel look fair an' fatter,
An' clear the consequential sorrows,
  Love-gifts of Carnival Signioras.
  For *Britain's guid*! for her destruction!
  Wi' dissipation, feud an' faction!

LUATH

Hech man! dear sirs! is that the gate,
They waste sae mony a braw estate!
Are we sae foughten an' harass'd
For gear to gang that gate at last!

O would they stay aback frae courts,
An' please themsels wi' countra sports,
It wad for ev'ry ane be better,
The *Laird*, the *Tenant*, an' the *Cotter*!
For thae frank, rantan, ramblan billies,
Fient haet o' them's illhearted fellows;
Except for breakin o' their *Limmer*,
Or shootin of a hare or moorcock,
The ne'er-a-bit they're ill to poor folk.

But will ye tell me, master *Ceasar*,
Sure *great folk's* life's a life o' pleasure?
Nae cauld nor hunger e'er can steer them,
The vera thought o't need na fear them.

CEASAR

Lord man, were ye but whyles where I am,
The *gentles* ye wad neer envy them!

It's true, they need na starve or sweat,
Thro' Winter's cauld, or Summer's heat;
They've nae sair-wark to craze their banes,
An' fill *auld-age* wi' grips an' granes:
But *human-bodies* are sic fools,
For a' their Colledges an' Schools,
That when nae *real* ills perplex them,
They *mak* enow themsels to vex them;
An' ay the less they hae to sturt them,
In like proportion, less will hurt them.

A country fellow at the pleugh,
His *acre's* till'd, he's right eneugh;
A country girl at her wheel,
Her *dizzen's* done, she's unco weel;
But Gentlemen, an' Ladies warst,
Wi' ev'n down *want o' wark* they're curst.
They loiter, lounging, lank an' lazy;
Tho' deil-haet ails them, yet uneasy;
Their days, insipid, dull an' tasteless,
Their nights, unquiet, lang an' restless.

An' ev'n their sports, their balls an' races,
Their galloping thro' public places,
There's sic parade, sic pomp an' art,
The joy can scarcely reach the heart.

The *Men* cast out in *party-matches,*
Then sowther a' in deep debauches.
Ae night, they're mad wi' drink an' wh-ring,
Niest day their life is past enduring.

The *Ladies* arm-in-arm in clusters,
As great an' gracious a' as sisters;
But hear their *absent thoughts* o' ither,
They're a' run-deils an' jads the gither.
Whyles, owre the wee bit cup an' platie,
They sip the *scandal-potion* pretty;
Or lee-lang nights, wi' crabbet leuks,
Pore owre the devil's *pictur'd beuks;*
Stake on a chance a farmer's stackyard,
An' cheat like ony *unhang'd blackguard.*

There's some exceptions, man an' woman;
But this is Gentry's life in common.

By this, the sun was out o' sight,
An' darker gloamin brought the night:
The *bum-clock* humm'd wi' lazy drone,
The kye stood rowtan i' the loan;
When up they gat, an' shook their lugs,
Rejoic'd they were na *men* but *dogs*;
An' each took off his several way,
Resolv'd to meet some ither day.

Address to the Deil

O Prince, O chief of many throned pow'rs,
That led th' embattl'd Seraphim to war—
MILTON

O THOU, whatever title suit thee!
Auld Hornie, Satan, Nick, or Clootie!
Wha in yon cavern grim an' sooty,
　　Clos'd under hatches,
Spairges about the brunstane cootie,
　　To scaud poor wretches!

Hear me, *auld Hangie*, for a wee,
An' let poor, *damned boides* bee;
I'm sure sma' pleasure it can gie,
　　Ev'n to a *deil*,
To skelp an' scaud poor dogs like me,
　　An' hear us squeel!

Great is thy pow'r, an' great thy fame;
Far ken'd, an' noted is thy name;
An' tho' yon *lowan heugh's* thy hame,
　　Thou travels far;
An' faith! thou's neither lag nor lame,
　　Nor blate nor scaur.

Whyles, ranging like a roaring lion,
For prey, a' holes an' corners tryin;
Whyles, on the strong-wing'd Tempest flyin,
　　Tirlan the *kirks*;
Whyles, in the human bosom pryin,
　　Unseen thou lurks.

I've heard my rev'rend *Graunie* say,
  In lanely glens ye like to stray;
Or where auld, ruin'd castles, gray,
    Nod to the moon,
Ye fright the nightly wand'rer's way,
    Wi' eldritch croon.

When twilight did my *Graunie* summon,
  To say her pray'rs, douse, honest woman,
Aft' yont the dyke she's heard you bumman,
    Wi' eerie drone;
Or, rustling, thro' the boortries coman,
    Wi' heavy groan.
Ae dreary, windy, winter night,

The stars shot down wi' sklentan light,
Wi' you, *mysel*, I gat a fright
Ayont the lough;
Ye, like a *rash-buss*, stood in sight,
Wi' waving sugh:

The cudgel in my nieve did shake,
Each bristl'd hair stood like a stake,
When wi' an eldritch, stoor *quaick, quaick*,
Amang the springs,
Awa ye squatter'd like a *drake*,
On whistling wings.

Let *Warlocks* grim, an' wither'd *Hags*,
Tell, how wi' you, on ragweed nags,
They skim the muirs an' dizzy crags,
Wi' wicked speed;
And in kirk-yards renew their leagues,
Owre howcket dead.

Thence, countra wives, wi' toil an' pain,
May plunge an' plunge the *kirn* in vain;
For Och! the yellow treasure's taen
By witching skill;
An' dawtit, twal-pint *Hawkie's* gane
As yell's the Bill.

Thence, mystic knots mak great abuse,
On *Young-Guidmen*, fond, keen an' croose;
When the best *warklum* i' the house,
By cantraip wit,
Is instant made no worth a louse,
Just at the bit.

When thowes dissolve the snawy hoord,

An' float the jinglan icy boord,
Then *Water-kelpies* haunt the foord,
By your direction,
An' nighted trav'llers are allur'd
To their destruction.

An' aft your moss-traversing *Spunkies*
Decoy the wight that late an' drunk is;
The bleezan, curst, mischievous monkies
Delude his eyes,
Till in some miry slough he sunk is,
Ne'er mair to rise.

When MASONS' mystic *word* an' *grip*,
In storms an' tempests raise you up,
Some cock, or cat, your rage maun stop,
Or, strange to tell!
The *youngest Brother* ye wad whip
Aff straught to *Hell*.

Lang syne in *Eden's* bonie yard,
When youthfu' lovers first were pair'd,
An' all the Soul of Love they shar'd,
The raptur'd hour,
Sweet on the fragrant, flow'ry swaird,
In shady bow'r:

Then you, ye auld, snick-drawing dog!
Ye cam to Paradise incog,
An' play'd on a man a cursed brogue,
(Black be your fa'!)
An' gied the infant warld a shog,
'Maist ruin'd a'.
D'ye mind that day, when in a bizz,

Wi reeket duds, an' reestet gizz,
Ye did present your smoutie phiz,
　　'Mang better folk,
An' sklented on the *man of Uz*,
　　Your spitefu' joke?

An' how ye gat him i' your thrall,
An' brak him out o' house an' hal',
While scabs an' botches did him gall,
　　Wi' bitter claw,
An' lows'd his ill-tongu'd, wicked *Scawl*
　　Was warst ava?

But a' your doings to rehearse,
Your wily snares an' fechtin fierce,
Sin' that day MICHAEL did you pierce,
　　Down to this time,
Wad ding a' *Lallan* tongue, or *Erse*,
　　In Prose or Rhyme.

An' now, auld *Cloots*, I ken ye're thinkan,
A certain *Bardie's* rantin, drinkin,
Some luckless hour will send him linkan,
　　To your black pit;
But faith! he'll turn a corner jinkan,
　　An' cheat you yet.

But fare you weel, auld *Nickie-ben*!
O wad ye tak a thought an' men'!
Ye aiblins might—I dinna ken—
　　Still hae a *stake*—
I'm wae to think upo' yon den,
　　Ev'n for your sake!

To a Louse, On Seeing One on a Lady's Bonnet at Church

HA! whare ye gaun, ye crowlan ferlie!
Your impudence protects you sairly:
I canna say but ye strunt rarely,
Owre *gawze* and *lace*;
Tho' faith, I fear ye dine but sparely,
On sic a place.

Ye ugly, creepan, blastet wonner,
Detested, shunn'd, by saunt an' sinner,
How daur ye set your fit upon her,
Sae fine a *Lady*!
Gae somewhere else and seek your dinner,
On some poor body.

Swith, in some beggar's haffet squattle;
There ye may creep, and sprawl, and sprattle,
Wi' ither kindred, jumping cattle,
In shoals and nations;
Whare *horn* nor *bane* ne'er daur unsettle,
Your thick plantations.

Now haud you there, ye're out o' sight,
Below the fatt'rels, snug and tight,
Na faith ye yet! ye'll no be right,
Till ye've got on it,
The vera tapmost, towrin height
O' *Miss's bonnet.*

My sooth! right bauld ye set your nose out,
As plump an' gray as onie grozet:
O for some rank, mercurial rozet,
Or fell, red smeddum,
I'd gie you sic a hearty dose o't,
Wad dress your droddum!

I wad na been surpriz'd to spy
You on an auld wife's *flainen toy*;
Or aiblins some bit duddie boy,
On's *wylecoat*;
But Miss's fine *Lundardi*, fye!
How daur ye do't?

O *Jenny* dinna toss your head,
An' set your beauties a' abread!
Ye little ken what cursed speed
The blastie's makin,
Thae *winks* and *finger-ends*, I dread,
Are notice takin!

O wad some Pow'r the giftie gie us
To see oursels as others see us!
It wad frae monie a blunder free us
An' foolish notion:
What airs in dress an' gait wad lea'e us,
And ev'n Devotion!

To a Mountain Daisy, On Turning One Down with the Plough in April, 1786

Wee, modest, crimson-tipped flow'r,
Thou's met me in an evil hour;
For I maun crush amang the stoure
Thy slender stem:
To spare thee now is past my pow'r,
Thou bonie gem.

Alas! it's no thy neebor sweet,
The bonie *lark*, companion meet!
Bending thee 'mang the dewy weet!
Wi' speckl'd breast,
When upward-springing, blythe, to greet
The purpling East.

Cauld blew the bitter-biting *North*
Upon thy early, humble birth;
Yet chearfully thou glinted forth
Amid the storm,
Scarce rear'd above the *Parent-earth*
Thy tender form.

The flaunting *flow'rs* our gardens yield,
High-shelt'ring woods and wa's maun shield,
But thou, beneath the random bield
O' clod or stane,
Adorns the histie *stibble-field*,
Unseen, alane.

There, in thy scanty mantle clad,
Thy snawy bosom sun-ward spread,
Thou lifts thy unassuming head
In humble guise;
But now the *share* uptears thy bed,
And low thou lies!

Such is the fate of artless Maid,
Sweet *flow'ret* of the rural shade!
By love's simplicity betray'd,
And guileless trust,
Till she, like thee, all soil'd, is laid
Low i' the dust.

Such is the fate of simple Bard,
On Life's rough ocean luckless starr'd!
Unskilful he to note the card
Of *prudent Lore*,
Till billows rage, and gales blow hard,
And whelm him o'er!

Such fate to *suffering worth* is giv'n,
Who long with wants and woes has striv'n,
By human pride or cunning driv'n
To Mis'ry's brink,
Till wrench'd of ev'ry stay but HEAV'N,
He, ruin'd, sink!

Ev'n thou who mourn'st the *Daisy's* fate,
That fate is thine—no distant date;
Stern Ruin's *plough-share* drives, elate,
Full on thy bloom,
Till crush'd beneath the *furrow's* weight,
Shall be thy doom!

Epitaph on a Henpecked Country Squire

As father Adam first was fool'd,
A case that's still too common,
Here lyes a man a woman rul'd,
The devil rul'd the woman.

Epigram on Said Occasion

O DEATH, hadst thou but spar'd his life,
 Whom we, this day, lament!
We freely wad exchang'd the *wife*,
 An' a' been weel content.

Ev'n as he is, cauld in his graff,
 The *swap* we yet will do't;
Tak thou the Carlin's carcase aff,
 Thou'se get the *saul o' boot*.

A Bard's Epitaph

IS THERE a whim-inspir'd fool,
Owre fast for thought, owre hot for rule,
Owre blate to seek, owre proud to snool,
Let him draw near;
And o'er this grassy heap sing dool,
And drap a tear.

Is there a Bard of rustic song,
Who, noteless, steals the crouds among,
That weekly this area throng,
O, pass not by!
But with a frater-feeling strong,
Here, heave a sigh.
Is there a man whose judgement clear,
Can others teach the course to steer,
Yet runs, himself, life's mad career,
Wild as the wave,
Here pause—and thro' the starting tear,
Survey this grave.

The poor Inhabitant below
Was quick to learn and wise to know,
And keenly felt the friendly glow,
And *softer flame*;
But thoughtless follies laid him low,
And stain'd his name!

Reader attend—whether thy soul
Soars fancy's flights beyond the pole,
Or darkling grubs this earthly hole,
In low pursuit,
Know, prudent, cautious, *self-controul*
Is Wisdom's root.

Address to a Haggis

FAIR FA' your honest, sonsie face,
Great Chieftan o' the Puddin-race!
Aboon them a' ye tak your place,
Painch, tripe, or thairm:
Weel are ye wordy of a *grace*
As lang's my arm.

The groaning trencher there ye fill,
Your hurdies like a distant hill,
Your *pin* wad help to mend a mill
In time o' need,
While thro' your pores the dews distil
Like amber bead.

His knife see Rustic-labour dight,
An' cut you up wi' ready slight,
Trenching your gushing entrails bright
Like onie ditch;
And then, O what a glorious sight,
Warm-reekin, rich!

Then, horn for horn they stretch an' strive,
Deil tak the hindmost, on they drive,
Till a' their weel-swall'd kytes belyve
Are bent like drums;
Then auld Guidman, maist like to rive,
Bethankit hums.

Is there that owre his French *ragout*,
 Or *olio* that wad staw a sow,
 Or *fricassee* wad mak her spew
  Wi' perfect sconner,
Looks down wi' sneering, scornfu' view
  On sic a dinner?

Poor devil! see him owre his trash,
 As feckless as a wither'd rash,
 His spindle shank a guid whip-lash,
  His nieve a nit;
Thro' bluidy flood or field to dash,
  O how unfit!

But mark the Rustic, *haggis-fed*,
The trembling earth resounds his tread,
 Clap in his walie nieve a blade,
  He'll mak it whissle;
An' legs, an' arms, an' heads will sned,
  Like taps o' thrissle.

Ye Pow'rs wha mak mankind your care,
 And dish them out their bill o' fare,
Auld Scotland wants nae skinking ware
  That jaups in luggies;
But, if ye wish her gratefu' pray'r,
  Gie her a *Haggis*!

Written with a Pencil, standing by the Fall of Fyers, near Loch-Ness

AMONG the heathy hills and ragged woods
The roaring Fyers pours his mossy floods;
Till full he dashes on the rocky mounds,
Where, thro' a shapeless breach, his stream resounds.
As high in air the bursting torrents flow,
As deep recoiling surges foam below,
Prone down the rock the whitening sheet descends,
And viewless Echo's ear, astonish'd, rends.
Dim-seen, through rising mists and ceaseless showers,
The hoary cavern, wide-surrounding, lowers.
Still thro' the gap the struggling river toils
And still, below, the horrid caldron boils—

The Winter it is Past

THE WINTER it is past, and the summer's come at last,
And the small birds sing on ev'ry tree;
The hearts of these are glad, but mine is very sad,
For my Lover has parted from me.

The rose upon the brier, by the waters running clear,
May have charms for the linnet or the bee;
Their little loves are blest and their little hearts at rest,
But my Lover is parted from me.

My love is like the sun, in the firmament does run,
For ever constant and true;
But his is like the moon that wanders up and down,
And every month it is new.

All you that are in love and cannot it remove,
I pity the pains you endure:
For experience makes me know that your hearts are full of
woe,
A woe that no mortal can cure.

Auld Lang Syne

SHOULD AULD acquaintance be forgot
And never brought to mind?
Should auld acquaintance be forgot,
And auld lang syne!

Chorus
For auld lang syne, my jo,
For auld lang syne,
We'll tak a cup o' kindness yet,
For auld lang syne.

And surely ye'll be your pint stowp!
And surely I'll be mine!
And we'll tak a cup o' kindness yet,
For auld lang syne.
For auld, &c.

We twa hae run about the braes,
And pou'd the gowans fine;
But we've wander'd mony a weary fitt,
Sin auld lang syne.
For auld, &c.

We twa hae paidl'd in the burn,
Frae morning sun till dine;
But seas between us braid hae roar'd,
Sin auld lang syne.
For auld, &c.

And there's a hand, my trusty fiere!
And gie's a hand o' thine!
And we'll tak a right gude-willie-waught,
For auld lang syne.

Caledonia

THERE WAS on a time, but old Time was then young,
 That brave Caledonia, the chief of her line,
 From some of your northern deities sprung,
 (Who knows not that brave Caledonia's divine)
 From Tweed to the Orcades was her domain,
 To hunt, or to pasture, or do what she would;
 Her heavenly relations there fixed her reign,
 And pledged their godheads to warrant it good.—

 A lambkin in peace, but a lion in war,
 The pride of her kindred the Heroine grew;
 Her grandsire, old Odin, triumphantly swore,
 'Who e'er shall provoke thee th' encounter shall rue!'
 With tillage or pasture at times she would sport,
 To feed her fair flocks by her green-rustling corn;
 But chiefly the woods were her fav'rite resort,
 Her darling amusement the hounds and the horn.—

 Long quiet she reigned, till thitherward steers
 A flight of bold eagles from Adria's strand;
 Repeated, successive, for many long years,
 They darkened the air and they plunder'd the land.
 Their pounces were murder, and horror their cry,
 They'd ravag'd and ruin'd a world beside;
 She took to her hills and her arrows let fly,
 The daring invaders they fled or they di'd.—
 The Camelon Savage disturb'd her repose

With tumult, disquiet, rebellion and strife;
Provok'd beyond bearing, at least she arose,
And robb'd him at once of his hopes and his life.
The Anglian lion, the terror of France,
Oft prowling ensanguin'd the Tweed's silver flood;
But taught by the bright Caledonian lance,
He learned to fear in his own native wood.—

The fell Harpy-raven took wing from the North,
The scourge of the seas and the dread of the shore;
The wild Scandinavian boar issu'd forth,
To wanton in carnage and wallow in gore:
O'er countries and kingdoms their fury prevail'd,
No arts could appease then, no arms could repel;
But brave Caledonia in vain they assail'd,
As Largs well can witness, and Loncartie tell.—

Thus bold, independant, unconquer'd and free,
Her bright course of glory for ever shall run;
For brave Caledonia immortal must be,
I'll prove it from Euclid as clear as the sun:
Rectangle-triangle the figure we'll chuse,
The Upright is Chance, and old Time is the Base;
But brave Caledonia's the Hypothenuse,
Then, Ergo, she'll match them, and match them always.

Afton Water

FLOW GENTLY, sweet Afton, among thy green braes,
Flow gently, I'll sing thee a song in thy praise;
My Mary's asleep by thy murmuring stream,
Flow gently, sweet Afton, disturb not her dream.

Thou stock dove whose echo resounds thro' the glen,
Ye wild whistling blackbirds in yon thorny den,
Thou green crested lapwing thy screaming forbear,
I charge you disturb not my slumbering Fair.

How lofty, sweet Afton, thy neighbouring hills,
Far mark'd with the courses of clear, winding rills;
There daily I wander as noon rises high,
My flocks and my Mary's sweet Cot in my eye.

How pleasant thy banks and green vallies below,
Where wild in the woodlands the primroses blow;
There oft as mild ev'ning weeps over the lea,
The sweet scented birk shades my Mary and me.

Thy chrystal stream, Afton, how lovely it glides,
And winds by the cot where my Mary resides;
How wanton thy waters her snowy feet lave,
As gathering sweet flowerets she stems thy clear wave.

Flow gently, sweet Afton, among thy green braes,
Flow gently, sweet River, the theme of my lays;
My Mary's asleep by thy murmuring stream,
Flow gently, sweet Afton, disturb not her dream.

ROBERT BURNS

My Heart's in the Highlands

MY HEART's in the Highlands, my heart is not here;
My heart's in the Highlands a chasing the deer;
Chasing the wild deer, and following the roe,
My heart's in the Highlands, wherever I go.–

Farewell to the Highlands, farewell to the North;
The birth place of Valour, the country of Worth:
Wherever I wander, wherever I rove,
The hills of the Highlands for ever I love.

Farewell to the mountains high cover'd with snow;
Farewell to the Straths and green vallies below:
Farewell to the forests and wild-hanging woods;
Farewell to the torrents and loud pouring floods.–

My heart's in the Highlands, my heart is not here,
My heart's in the Highlands a chasing the deer:
Chasing the wild deer, and following the roe,
My heart's in the Highlands, wherever I go.–

Tam o' Shanter. A Tale

Of Brownyis and of Bogillis full is this buke.
GAWIN DOUGLAS

WHEN CHAPMAN billies leave the street,
And drouthy neebors, neebors meet,
As market-days are wearing late,
An' folk begin to tak the gate;
While we sit bousing at the nappy,
And getting fou and unco happy,
We think na on the lang Scots miles,
The mosses, waters, slaps and styles,
That lie between us and our hame,
Whare sits our sulky sullen dame,
Gathering her brows like gathering storm,
Nursing her wrath to keep it warm.

This truth fand honest *Tam o' Shanter*,
As he frae Ayr ae night did canter,
(Auld Ayr, wham ne'er a town surpasses,
For honest men and bonny lasses.)

O *Tam*! hadst thou but been sae wise,
As ta'en thy ain wife *Kate's* advice!
She tauld thee weel thou was a skellum,
A blethering, blustering, drunken blellum;
That frae November till October,
Ae market day thou was nae sober;
That ilka melder, wi' the miller,
Thou sat as lang as thou had siller;
That every naig was ca'd a shoe on,
The smith and thee gat roaring fou on;

That at the Lord's house, even on Sunday,
Thou drank wi' Kirkton Jean till Monday.
She prophesied that late or soon,
Thou would be found deep drown'd in Doon;
Or catch'd wi' warlocks in the mirk,
By *Alloway's* auld haunted kirk.

Ah, gentle dames! it gars me greet,
To think how mony counsels sweet,
How mony lengthen'd, sage advices,
The husband frae the wife despises!

But to our tale: Ae market night,
Tam had got planted unco right;
Fast by an ingle, bleezing finely,
Wi' reaming swats, that drank divinely;
And at his elbow, Souter *Johnny*,
His ancient, trusty, drouthy crony;
Tam lo'ed him like a vera brither;
They had been fou for weeks thegither.
The night drave on wi' sangs and clatter;
And ay the ale was growing better:
The landlady and *Tam* grew gracious,
Wi' favours, secret, sweet, and precious:
The Souter tauld his queerest stories;
The landlord's laugh was ready chorus:
The storm without might rair and rustle,
Tam did na mind the storm a whistle.

Care, mad to see a man sae happy,
E'en drown'd himsel amang the nappy:
As bees flee hame wi' lades o' treasure,
The minutes wing'd their way wi' pleasure:
Kings may be blest, but *Tam* was glorious,

O'er a' the ills o' life victorious!

But pleasures are like poppies spread,
You seize the flower, its bloom is shed;
Or like the snow falls in the river,
A moment white – then melts for ever;
Or like the borealis race,
That flit ere you can point their place;
Or like the rainbow's lovely form
Evanishing amid the storm. –
Nae man can tether time nor tide;
The hour approaches *Tam* maun ride;
That hour, o' night's black arch the key-stane,
That dreary hour he mounts his beast in;
And sic a night he taks the road in,
As ne'er poor sinner was abroad in.

The wind blew as 'twad blawn its last;
The rattling showers rose on the blast;
The speedy gleams the darkness swallow'd;
Loud, deep, and lang, the thunder bellow'd:
That night, a child might understand,
The Deil had business on his hand.

Weel mounted on his gray mare, *Meg*,
A better never lifted leg,
Tam skelpit on thro' dub and mire,
Despising wind, and rain, and fire;
Whiles holding fast his gude blue bonnet;
Whiles crooning o'er some auld Scots sonnet;
Whiles glowring round wi' prudent cares,
Lest bogles catch him unawares:
Kird-Alloway was drawing nigh,
Whare ghaists and houlets nightly cry. –

By this time he was cross the ford,
Whare, in the snaw, the chapman smoor'd;
And past the birks and meikle stane,
Whare drunken *Charlie* brak's neck-bane;
And thro' the whins, and by the cairn,
Whare hunters fand the murder'd bairn;
And near the thorn, aboon the well,
Whare *Mungo's* mither hang'd hersel. –
Before him *Doon* pours all his floods:
The doubling storm roars thro' the woods:
The lightnings flash from pole to pole;
Near and more near the thunders roll:
When, glimmering thro' the groaning trees,
   Kirk-Alloway seem'd in a bleeze;
Thro' ilka bore the beams were glancing;
And loud resounded mirth and dancing. –

Inspiring bold *John Barleycorn*!
What dangers thou canst make us scorn!
   Wi' tippenny, we fear nae evil;
   Wi' usquabae we'll face the devil! –
The swats sae ream'd in *Tammie's* noddle,
Fair play, he car'd na deils a boddle.
But *Maggie* stood right sair astonish'd,
Till, by the heel and hand admonish'd,
   She ventured forward on the light;
And, vow! *Tam* saw an unco sight!
Warlocks and witches in a dance;
Nae cotillion brent new frae *France*,
But hornpipes, jigs, strathspeys, and reels,
Put life and mettle in their heels.
   A winnock-bunker in the east,
There sat auld Nick, in shape o' beast;
A towzie tyke, black, grim, and large,

To gie them music was his charge:
He screw'd the pipes and gart them skirl,
Till roof and rafters a' did dirl. –
Coffins stood round, like open presses,
That shaw'd the dead in their last dresses;
And by some devilish cantraip slight
Each in its cauld hand held a light. –
By which heroic *Tam* was able
To note upon the haly table,
A murderer's banes in gibbet airns;
Twa span-lang, wee, unchristen'd bairns;
A thief, new-cutted frae a rape,
Wi' his last gasp his gab did gape;
Five tomahawks, wi' blude red-rusted;
Five scymitars, wi' murder crusted;
A garter, which a babe had strangled;
A knife, a father's throat had mangled,
Whom his ain son o' life bereft,
The grey hairs yet stack to the heft;
Wi' mair o' horrible an' awefu',
Which even to name wad be unlawfu'.

As *Tammie* glow'rd, amaz'd, and curious,
The mirth and fun grew fast and furious:
The piper loud and louder blew;
The dancers quick and quicker flew;
They reel'd, they set, they cross'd, they cleekit,
Till ilka carlin swat and reekit,
And coost her duddies to the wark,
And linket at it in her sark!

Now *Tam*, O *Tam*! had thae been queans,
A' plump and strapping in their teens,
Their sarks, instead o' creeshie flannen,

Been snaw-white seventeen hunder linnen!
Thir breeks o' mine, my only pair,
That ance were plush, o' gude blue hair,
I wad hae gi'en them off my hurdies,
For ae blink o' the bonie burdies!

But wither'd beldams, auld and droll,
Rigwoodie hags wad spean a foal,
Lowping and flinging on a crummock,
I wonder didna turn thy stomach.

But Tam kend what was what fu' brawlie,
There was ae winsome wench and wawlie,
That night enlisted in the core,
(Lang after kend on Carrick shore;
For mony a beast to dead she shot,
And perish'd mony a bony boat,
And shook baith meikle corn and bear,
And kept the country-side in fear:)
Her cutty sark, o' Paisley harn,
That while a lassie she had worn,
In longitude tho' sorely scanty,
It was her best, and she was vauntie. —
Ah! little kend thy reverend grannie,
That sark she coft for her wee Nannie,
Wi' twa pund Scots ('twas a' her riches)
Wad ever grac'd a dance o' witches!

But here my Muse her wing maun cour;
Sic flights are far beyond her pow'r;
To sing how Nannie lap and flang,
(A souple jade she was, and strang),
And how Tam stood, like ane bewitch'd,
And thought his very een enrich'd;

Even Satan glowr'd, and fidg'd fu' fain,
And hotch'd and blew wi' might and main:
Till first ae caper, syne anither,
Tam tint his reason a' thegither,
And roars out, 'Weel done, Cutty-sark!'
And in an instant all was dark:
And scarcely had he Maggie rallied,
When out the hellish legion sallied.

As bees bizz out wi' angry fyke,
When plundering herds assail their byke,
As open pussie's mortal foes,
When pop! she starts before their nose;
As eager runs the market-crowd,
When 'Catch the thief!' resounds aloud;
So Maggie runs, the witches follow,
Wi' mony an eldritch skreech and hollow.

Ah, *Tam*! Ah, *Tam*! thou'll get thy fairin!
In hell they'll roast thee like a herrin!
In vain thy *Kate* awaits thy comin!
Kate soon will be a woefu' woman!
Now, do thy speedy utmost, Meg,
And win the key-stane of the brig;
There at them thou thy tail may toss,
A running stream they dare na cross.
But ere the key-stane of the brig;
There at them thou thy tail may toss,
A running stream they dare na cross.
But ere the key-stane she could make,
The fient a tale she had to shake!
For Nannie, far before the rest,
Hard upon noble Maggie prest,
And flew at *Tam* wi' furious ettle;

But little wist she Maggie's mettle —
Ae spring brought off her master hale,
But left behind her ain gray tail:
The carlin claught her by the rump,
And left poor Maggie scarce a stump.

Now, wha this tale o' truth shall read,
Ilk man and mother's son, take heed:
Whene'er to drink you are inclin'd,
Or cutty-sarks run in your mind,
Think, ye may buy the joys o'er dear,
Remember Tam o' Shanter's mare.

What Can a Young Lassie do wi' an Auld Man

WHAT CAN a young lassie, what shall a young lassie,
    What can a young lassie do wi' an auld man?
Bad luck on the pennie, that tempted my Minnie
    To sell her poor Jenny for siller and lan'!

He's always compleenin frae morning to e'enin,
    He hosts and he hirpels the weary day lang:
He's doyl't and he's dozin, his blude it is frozen,
    O, dreary's the night wi' a crazy auld man!

He hums and he hankers, he frets and he cankers,
    I never can please him, do a' that I can;
He's peevish, and jealous of a' the young fallows,
    O, dool on the day I met wi' an auld man!

My auld auntie Katie upon me taks pity,
    I'll do my endeavour to follow her plan;
I'll cross him, and wrack him untill I heartbreak him,
    And then his auld brass will buy me a new pan.—

ROBERT BURNS

Comin thro' the Rye

COMIN thro' the rye, poor body,
Comin thro' they rye,
She draigl't a' her petticoatie
Comin thro the rye.

Oh Jenny's a' weet, poor body,
Jenny's seldom dry;
She draigl't a' her petticoatie
Comin thro' the rye.

Gin a body meet a body
Comin' thro' the rye,
Gin a body kiss a body
Need a body cry.

Chorus: O Jenny's a' weet, &c.

Gin a body meet a body
Comin thro' the glen;
Gin a body kiss a body
Need the warld ken!

Chorus: O Jenny's a' weet &c.

Glossary

a'	all	braid-cloth	broad-cloth
aboon	above	braw	gaily dressed,
abread	abroad		handsome
ae	one	breeks	breeches
aff	off	brunstane	brimstone
aff-han(d)	at once	bum	to hum
aft	oft	bum-cock	a humming beetle
agley	wrong	burd(ie)	lady, girl
aiblins	maybe, perhaps	byke, bike	swarm, crowd
ain	own		
air	early	ca'	to call, drive cattle
amaist	almost	caller	cool, fresh
amang	among	cam	came
ance	once	ca(n)ie	gentle, prudent
ane	one	cantie	lively, cheerful
anither	another	cantraip	magic, witching
aught	eight, anything	cauld	cold
auld	old	caup	wooden drinking
ava	at all, of all		vessel
awa	away	chantan	singing
ayon	beyond	chapman	a pedlar
		cheel, chiel	lad, young fellow
bairn	child	claes	clothes
baith	both	clankie	knock, blow
bane	bone	cloot	hoof
bauld	bold	coost	cast, threw off
bead	drop of liquor	cootie	wooden dish
bear	barley	cotillion	French dance
beld	bald	cour	to lower, fold
belyve	by-and-by, soon	cranreuch	hoar-frost
beuk	book	creeshie	greasy, filthy
biel(d)	shelter	croose, crouse	cocksure, merry
billie	comrade, lad	crowlan	creeping
birkie	lively fellow	curchie	curtsey
blastet	blasted	cutty	short, brief
blate	bashful		
bleeze	blaze	daffin	frolic, flirtation
blellum	idle babbler	dail	plank of wood
boddle	copper coin	daur	daredaut
body	a person, creature	dawt(e)	fondle, pet
bogle	ghost, goblin	dawd	hunk, large piece
bonie	fair, pretty	deil, deevil	devil
bouk	body, carcass	deu(c)k	duck
bowse	drink, booze	did(d)ie	more jerkily,
brae	small hill		fiddle

dine	dinner	*ghaist*	ghost
ding	to beat, overcome	*gie*	to give
dinna	do not	*gin*	if, should, whether
dirl	to rattle, shake	*giz(z)*	wig
diz(ze)n	dozen	*glow'r*	stare wide-eyed
doited	muddled	*graith*	tools, gear, attire
donsie	unlucky	*grozet*	gooseberry
dool	sorrow, misery	*grushie*	thriving ,strong
douce, douse	sober, kindly	*gude, guid*	good
doytan	stumbling, blundering	*gude-willie*	full of good-will
drap	drop	*ha'*	hall
drouthy	thirsty	*ha' folk*	servants
drumlie	cloudy, gloomy	*hae, ha'(e)*	have
duddie	ragged, tattered	*hafflins*	half, partly
dud(d)ies	clothes, rags	*haith*	a petty oath
		haly	holy
e'e	eye	*hame*	home
e'en	evening	*han-daurk*	labour of the hands
e'en	even, just	*hause*	embrace
eldritch	uncanny, fearsome haunted	*heugh*	crag, steep bank
		hirple	to limp, to hobble
		histie	bear, stony
fa'	a portion, a lot	*hizzie*	a hussy, wench
fa'	to fall, come by	*hornie*	the devil
fae	foe	*houlet*	owl
fain o' ither	fond of each other	*how(c)kt*	to dig, delve
fash	to trouble, bother	*hurdies*	buttocks, backside
fatt'rels	ribbon-ends		
faut	fault	*ilk(a)*	each, every
fawsont	respectable	*indentin*	pledging, engaging
fecht	to fight	*ingle*	the fire, the fireplace
feck	the majority, most		
ferlie	a wonder (contemptuous)	*ither*	other, one another
ferlie	to marvel	*jad*	a jade
flainen	flannel	*jaup*	splash,
fou	full, drunk	*jo(e)*	sweetheart
frae	from		
fu'	full	*kane*	payment in kind
furm	wooden bench	*kebbuck*	a cheese
fyke	to defile, foul	*keek*	to look, peep
		kelpie	water demon in shape of horse
gab	mouth, jaw		
gae	to go, walk	*ken*	to know
gaets	habits, manners	*kirk*	church
gar	to cause, make	*kirn*	a churn
gash	shrewd, witty	*kittle*	to rouse
gausie, gawsy	jolly, buxom	*kye*	cows, cattle
gawkie	fool	*kyte*	belly
gear	possessions, money	*laird*	landowner

laith	loath, unwilling		
lang	long	*quean*	young girl
lang syne	long since, ancient		
lave	the rest, the	*raep, rape*	rope
	remainder	*raible*	to gabble
leeze me on	I am delighted by	*rair*	to roar
leuk	to look, to watch	*rant*	make merry
limmer	a jade, a mistress	*rash*	a rush
loan	a field path	*ream*	froth, foam
lo'ed	loved	*reck*	to heed
lug	ear	*red(e)*	counsel, advice
lunt	to smoke a pipe	*reeket*	smoked, smokey
lyart	streaked with white	*reestit*	singed, cured
		rive	to split, pull asunder
Mailie	Molly	*rozet*	resin
mair	more, greater	*runkl'd*	wrinkled
maist(ly)	mostly		
maist	almost	*sae*	so
'mang	among	*saft*	soft
maun	must	*sair*	sore, heavy, harsh
meikle, mu(c)kle	much, great	*sark*	shirt, chemise
melder	quantity of corn	*scar*	to frighten off
	for grinding	*scawl*	to scold
mim	demure, prim	*sconner*	disgust, revulsion
mither	mother	*screed*	a tear, a rip
monie, mony	many	*sheugh*	trench, ditch
muir	moor	*shog*	a shock, a shake
		sic	such
na(e)	no, not	*siller*	wealth, silver
naething	nothing	*simmer*	summer
nappy	strong ale	*sin'*	since
neuk, newk	corner, recess	*skellum*	a rascal, scoundrel
niest, neist	next	*skinking*	watery
nieve	the fist	*skirl*	a shriek, a yell
niffer	an exchange	*sleeket*	smooth, glossy
noddle	head, brain	*sma'*	small, slight
		smeddum	a fine powder
o'	of	*smeek*	smoke
onie	any	*smiddie*	smithy
owre	over	*smoor'd*	smothered
		smoutie	smutty
painch	belly, paunch	*smytrie*	a large collection
pattle	spade for cleaning	*snash*	abuse
	plough	*sned*	to cut off
peghan	the stomach	*snood*	a girl's hair-band
penny-wheep	a small beer	*snowck*	to snuff, poke
phiz	the face		about with the
pictur'd beuk	a playing card		nose
plaister	plaster	*sonsie*	good-natured
pleugh	plough	*sowther*	to solder, patch up
poind	to seize goods	*spairge*	to sprinke, bespatter

splore	a frolic, an uproar
spunkie	will-o'-the wisp
squattle	to squat, nestle down
stan'	to stand, to stop
stane	stone
stegh	to cram the tomach
stent	tax, duty
stoure	storm, dust
stroan't	pissed
strunt	to strut
sturt	to fret
sugh	a sigh, a moan
swith	quickly! away!
taen	taken
thack	thatching
thairm	intestine
thrang	crowd
thrissle	thistle
tirl	to uncover, to rattle
towsie	unkempt, shaggy
thrashtrie	rubbish, trash
twa'	two
tyke	a dog
unco	remarkable, strange
unkenn'd	unknown
usquabae	whisky
vauntie	vain
vera	very
wad	would, would have
wae	woeful, sorrowful
wae sucks!	alas
walie	robust, handsome
wastrie	wastefulness, extravagance
weel	well, fine
whase	whose
whalp	whelp
whare	where
whipper-in	huntsman who controls hounds
whunstane	whinstone, hard rock
whyles	sometimes
wi'	with

wight	creature, fellow
wonner	a marvel (often contemptuous)
wylecoat	a flannel vest
yestreen	last night
yill	ale
yowe	ewe

Index of First Lines

Notes on Illustrations

3   *Robert Burns (Chalk)* by Archibald Skirving (Scottish National Portrait Gallery, Edinburgh). Courtesy of The Bridgeman Art Library.

7   *Robert Burns* by Alexander Nasmyth (Scottish National Portrait Gallery, Edinburgh). Courtesy of The Bridgeman Art Library.

8   *The Last Gleam* by Walter Fryer Stocks (Victoria & Albert Museum, London). Courtesy of The Bridgeman Art Library.

11   *The Parliament Close* by Roberts, Wilkie, Nasmyth & Stanfield (City of Edinburgh Museums & Art Galleries, Edinburgh). Courtesy of City of Edinburgh Museums & Art Galleries.

17   *A Shepherdess with Her Dog & Flock in a Moonlit Meadow* by George Faulkner Wetherbee (Christie's, London). Courtesy of The Bridgeman Art Library.

18-19 *Scottish Highlands* by Clarence Roe (Oscar & Peter Johnson Ltd., London). Courtesy of The Bridgeman Art Library.

23   *The Rescue* by Richard Ansdell (Malcolm Innes Gallery, London). Courtesy of The Bridgeman Art Library.

25   *The Flea* by Giuseppe Maria Crespi (Galleria Degli Offizi, Florence). Courtesy of The Bridgeman Art Library.

27   *The Hireling Shepherd* by William Holman Hunt (Manchester City Art Galleries). Courtesy of The Bridgeman Art Library.

36   *The Death of the Red Deer* by Sir David Wilkie (Christie's, London). Courtesy of The Bridgeman Art Library.

38   *Disbanded* by John Pettite (City of Dundee District Council, Dundee). Courtesy of MacManus Galleries.

46   *The Satyrs and the Family* by Jan Havicksz Steen (Rafael Valls Gallery, London). Courtesy of The Bridgeman Art Library.

52   *Among The Flowers.* Courtesy of The Laurel Clark Collection, Tunbridge Wells, Kent.

56   *A Piper of the 79th Highlanders at Chobham Camp in 1853* by Eugene-Louis Lami (Victoria & Albert Museum, London). Courtesy of The Bridgeman Art Library.

59   *Collecting the Offering in a Scottish Church* by John Phillip (York City Art Gallery). Courtesy of The Bridgeman Art Library.

63   *The Falls of the Clyde after a Flood* by James Ward (The Fine Art Society, London). Courtesy of The Bridgeman Art Library.

64-5 *Ben Venue in the Trossachs* by Thomas Miles Richardson (Malcolm Innes Gallery, London). Courtesy of The Bridgeman Art Library.

69   *The Highland Shepherd* by Rosa Bonheur (Bury Art Gallery & Museum). Courtesy of The Bridgeman Art Library.

71   *A Highland River Landscape* by Daniel Sherrin (Christopher Wood Gallery, London). Courtesy of The Bridgeman Art Library.

72-3 *A Highland Loch Scene* by Sidney Richard Percy (Bonhams, London). Courtesy of The Bridgeman Art Library.

80-1 *For Better or Worse - Rob Roy and the Baillie* by John Watson Nichol (Sheffield City Art Galleries). Courtesy of The Bridgeman Art Library.

85   *A Warming Brew* by Edwin Thomas Roberts. Courtesy of Fine Art Photographic Library Ltd.

86-7 *Harvesting* by John Clayton Adams. Courtesy of Fine Art Photographic Library Ltd.

92-3 *'For Auld Lang Syne – A Right Merry Christmas'*, Early 20th-century Postcard (Private Collection). Courtesy of The Bridgeman Art Library.

DATE DUE

MAY 19 2004			
JUN 02 2004			
SEP 09 2004			
JAN 24 2006			
JAN 23 2007			
Feb 2 2007			
AUG 15 2011			

DEMCO 38-297